What a Job

Be Brave!

by Wiley Blevins

I0869460

LOOK! BOOKS™

Red Chair Press Egremont, Massachusetts

Look! Books are produced and published by Red Chair Press:
Red Chair Press LLC PO Box 333 South Egremont, MA 01258-0333

FREE Educator Guides at www.redchairpress.com/free-resources

Publisher's Cataloging-In-Publication Data

Names: Blevins, Wiley, author.

Title: Be brave! / by Wiley Blevins.

Description: Egremont, Massachusetts : Red Chair Press, [2021] | Series: Look! books : What a job | Interest age level: 005-008. | Includes index and resources for additional reading. | Summary: "In this book readers discover careers that require the worker to be brave and often to help others, such as firefighters and police officers"--Provided by publisher.

Identifiers: ISBN 9781634408288 (library hardcover) | ISBN 9781634408325 (paperback) | ISBN 9781634408363 (ebook)

Subjects: LCSH: Fire fighters--Vocational guidance--Juvenile literature. | Public safety--Vocational guidance--Juvenile literature. | Courage--Juvenile literature. | CYAC: Fire fighters--Vocational guidance. | Public safety--Vocational guidance. | Courage.

Classification: LCC HD8039.F5 B54 2021 (print) | LCC HD8039.F5 (ebook) | DDC 363.37023 [E]--dc23

Photo credits: iStock except for the following: pp. 1, 11, 16, 17, 21: Shutterstock; p. 5: Barrett & MacKay/Alamy

Printed in United States of America

0920 1P CGS21

Table of Contents

A person must be brave to do these jobs. To be brave means to have no fear. Are you brave enough?

Smokejumper

A big fire races through the forest. Who comes to help? Smokejumpers! They jump out of a plane. Where to? Into the middle of the fire. They carry special **equipment.** They use it to fight the fires.

Good to Know

Smokejumpers need boots, a knife, jumpsuit, and a good parachute.

These brave workers use a parachute to jump into the fire.

Storm Chaser

A tornado or hurricane is coming. Most people run inside to keep safe. Not storm chasers! They run toward the bad weather. Why? Storm chasers study storms. They **warn** people of danger. They risk their lives to save ours.

Storm chasers use special equipment to tell us where storms are moving.

Window Washer

Big buildings have lots of windows. How do they get cleaned? Window washers do it. They sit in a special chair. Where? Outside the building. Then they use ropes to go up, up, up. Be brave, don't look down!

Nurse

Nurses help people stay healthy. They also care for people who are sick or hurt. That means they can get very sick themselves. But they are still always ready with a smile! Nurses often work long hours in hospitals.

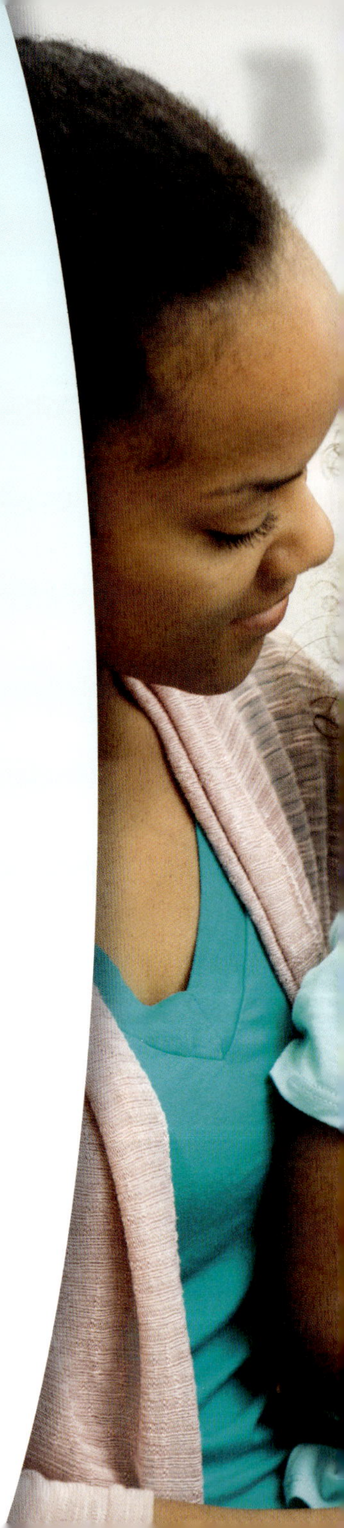

Nurses often wear special things like masks and gloves to protect themselves from getting sick.

Snake Milker

Most people are afraid of snakes. Not on this job. These workers milk snakes. The kind that can kill! They don't really get milk. They get the snake's **venom**. That is what can kill you.

Snake milkers use the venom to make medicines. The medicines can save people's lives. The milkers work in a place where lots of snakes live. It is called a *serpentarium*. Snake milkers are a kind of scientist.

Good to Know

Milking venom from snakes does not hurt the snakes.

Cobras, rattlesnakes, and copperheads are some of the snakes workers milk for venom.

Beekeeper

Buzz. Buzz. Buzz. Bees fly all around on this job. These workers keep beehives. Why? Bees are important. They help to **pollinate** plants. Bees must do this for plants to grow fruits and vegetables.

Beekeepers need special clothes. The clothes help them to not get stung. They also use a smoker to calm the bees. They sell the bee's yummy honey to make money.

Good to Know

Bees pollinate flowers in the spring and summer. They eat their honey in winter to stay alive.

Rescue Worker

Call 9-1-1. It's an emergency! Who will come? A rescue worker. These workers are the first to show up after a **disaster** like an earthquake. They work fast to save lives.

There are many kinds of rescue workers. Some drive ambulances. Some work with special dogs to find people trapped under buildings. All are brave!

Words to Know

disaster: a sudden event that causes loss of life or lots of damage

equipment: anything used for a specific purpose on the job

pollinate: to put pollen on a flower

venom: poison liquid in an animal, like a snake

warn: to tell of upcoming danger

Learn More at the Library

Check out these books to learn more.

Nargi, Lela. *The Honeybee Man.* Schwartz & Wade, 2011.

O'Shei, Tim. *The World's Most Dangerous Jobs.* Capstone Press, 2007.

Paul, Miranda. *Whose Hands Are These?* (Community Helpers). Millbrook Press, 2016.

Index

About the Author

Wiley Blevins works with words all day. He is on the job as a writer and editor in New York. He does not have to be brave to do his job, but he must be smart.